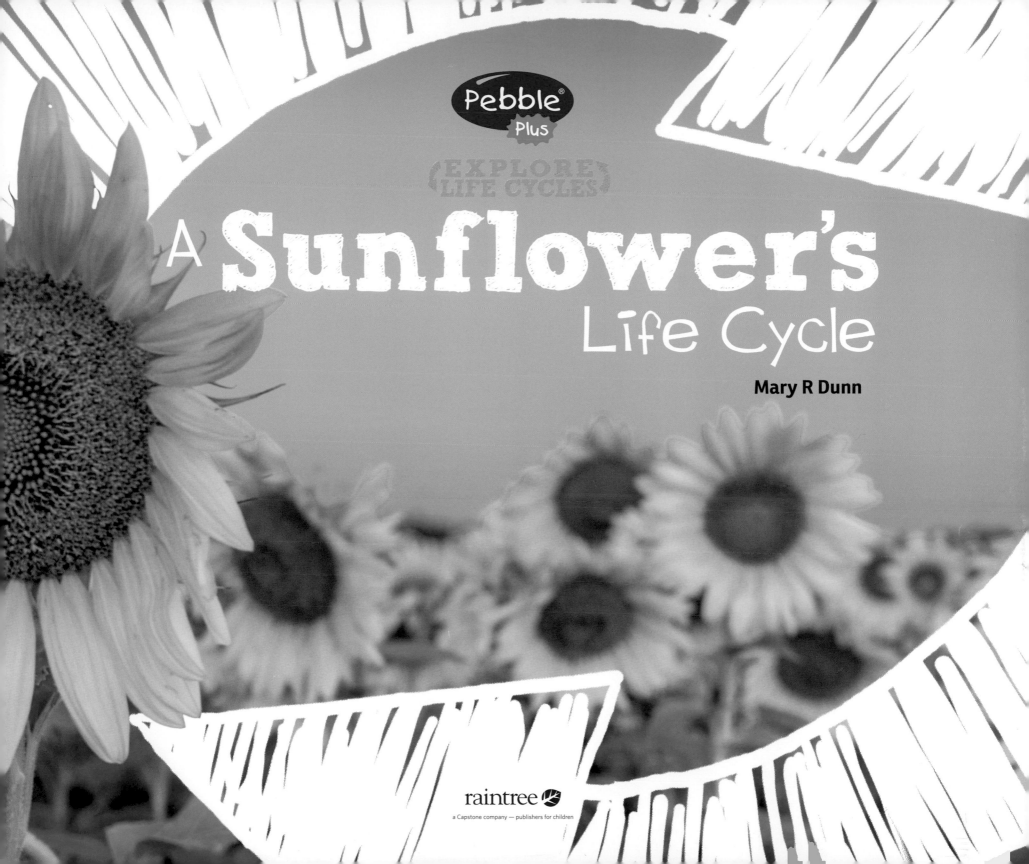

Pebble® Plus

EXPLORE LIFE CYCLES

# A Sunflower's
## Life Cycle

**Mary R Dunn**

raintree

a Capstone company — publishers for children

Raintree is an imprint of Capstone Global Library Limited, a company incorporated in England and Wales having its registered office at 264 Banbury Road, Oxford, OX2 7DY – Registered company number: 6695582

www.raintree.co.uk
myorders@raintree.co.uk

Edited by Anna Butzer
Designed by Kyle Grenz
Picture research by Wanda Winch
Production by Kathy McColley
Originated by Capstone Global Library Ltd
Printed and bound in China

ISBN 978 1 4747 4327 3
21 20 19 18 17
10 9 8 7 6 5 4 3 2 1

**British Library Cataloguing in Publication Data**
A full catalogue record for this book is available from the British Library.

**Acknowledgements**
We would like to thank the following for permission to reproduce photographs: Shutterstock: AMC Images, 1, Bogdan Wankowicz, 5, 7, boyphare, 19, dimid_86, 21, Emilio100, 9, Helen's Photos, 15, Jerry Lin, 11, Narudom Chaisuwon, cover, NattapolStudiO, 17, Samiran Sarker, sunflower silhouette, SJ Travel Photo and Video, back cover, Yuthana Choradet, 13

Every effort has been made to contact copyright holders of material reproduced in this book. Any omissions will be rectified in subsequent printings if notice is given to the publisher.

All the internet addresses (URLs) given in this book were valid at the time of going to press. However, due to the dynamic nature of the internet, some addresses may have changed, or sites may have changed or ceased to exist since publication. While the author and publisher regret any inconvenience this may cause readers, no responsibility for any such changes can be accepted by either the author or the publisher.

# Contents

# A flower seed

Pop! Under the warm spring soil

a seed breaks open.

It will grow to be a tall plant

with yellow flowers.

It is a sunflower seed.

The seed sends out roots.

Roots push deep into the soil.

They take in water and minerals.

A green shoot pokes out of the soil.

# Sprouting leaves

The shoot becomes the plant's stem.

The first leaves sprout from the stem.

Leaves use water, sunlight and air

to make food for the plant.

9

Tiny hairs cover the stem.

The hairs stop insects from climbing

up the stem and eating the leaves.

More leaves grow on the stem.

# Growing tall

The stem grows taller and taller.

Some may grow over

3 metres (12 feet) high. Wow!

Green leaves called bracts

form on the flower bud.

13

As the bracts unfold, yellow flower petals poke out. The petals open and the flower head grows bigger.

# Blooming flowers

Sunflower heads have

hundreds of tiny florets.

Florets are covered with pollen dust.

Bees land on the bright florets.

Bees land on many sunflowers,

spreading pollen among the florets.

Florets have tiny ovules.

Pollen and ovules form new seeds.

19

In the autumn, some sunflower seeds are harvested. Other seeds fall to the ground. They will grow into new plants in spring.

# GLOSSARY

**bract**  part of a plant that protects the bud while it grows

**floret**  tiny flower that is part of a flower head

**flower head**  flower that is made up of many tiny florets

**harvest**  gather in ripe crops

**mineral**  chemical that the plant needs to stay healthy

**ovule**  female egg that joins with male pollen to form a seed

**petal**  small colorful part of a flower

**pollen**  tiny male parts of a plant

**root**  part of a plant that grows under the ground and takes in water

**shoot**  white stem growing out of a seed that becomes a plant

**soil**  top layer of ground where plants grow

**stem**  part of a plant that connects the roots to the leaves

# FIND OUT MORE

## BOOKS

*Lifecycles* (Ways into Science), Peter Riley (Franklin Watts, 2016)

*Sunflower* (Life Cycles), Ruth Thomson (Wayland, 2013)

*The Amazing Plant Life* Cycle Story, Kay Barnham (Wayland, 2017)

## WEBSITES

www.bbc.co.uk/education/clips/z3wsbk7
Learn about the life cycle of a plant in this video.

www.rhs.org.uk/education-learning/gardening-children-schools/family-activities/grow-it/grow/sunflower
Grow your own sunflowers! Ask a grown-up to help you follow the steps on this web page.

# COMPREHENSION QUESTIONS

1. How do roots help the sunflower to grow?

2. Why is it hard for insects to eat sunflower leaves?

3. Find the word in the glossary that tells where plants grow.

# INDEX